This journal belongs to

_____

Wellness
journal
___

This beautiful wellness journal will help you to express your feelings and thoughts.

The prompted questions throughout is designed to help you identify the different thought patterns, trigger points to help you challenge those anxious/worry thoughts and exchange them for **positive** and **intentional** actions.

The daily selfcare questions throughout will help you to track your habits, menu, health/wellbeing and reflect on each day's achievements.

The journey of a 100 miles begins with the first step. Enjoy the journey..

Wellness journal

Selfcare Isn't Selfish

My selfcare Goals

Write down all your goals for each category

Physical
Be more active as working from home. love my body.

Relationship
Spend more family time together. Spend more time with the kids. Spend time as sara + greg.

Emotional
love my body. Don't guilt trip myself. Stop waiting for something bad to happen

Mental
To NOT over think. Not let my negative mind control me

Financial
NO Debt. to be guilt free for me + G to treat our selfs. more chances for family adventures

Health
help my healthy bones. Eat better. Cut out sugar. Sort teeth look after me.

Plan of action

_____

_____

_____

_____

Vision & ideas
at a glance

- holiday
- new job ✓
- pals
- be me ✓
- eat better ✓
- eat more ✓
- sleep better
- yoga
- adventure
- Bike
- make friends
- learn new thing
- family time
- mom stuff
- men £?
- keys
- car
- save £
- Diva
- learn new thing
- house
- Pets

Worry jar

Use this jar to write down each worry on your mind. Revisit the jar at least once a week and pick one out and focus on how you can tackle it. Do this by writing it out in the tracker page and think of different ways to address it.

Worry Tracker

I'm worried about...	Suggested solutions Who? What? How?	Achieved Y/N (date)
Not doing enough		

Notes

Inhale the future
exhale the past

Daily Wellness Journal

Date: 18 / 1 /20 22   Sun   Mon   (Tue)   Wed   Thu   Fri   Sat

GRATEFUL for: My Amazing husband, keeping things going during my training

Today I CHOOSE TO FEEL
Positive

Today's GOOD HABITS
Still cutting out 2 sugars.

Things I do well
- [ ] laughing with my
- [ ] 1.
- [ ] Staying upbeat
- [ ]
- [ ]
- [ ]

Self-Care
- [ ] yoga
- [ ] breathing excercise
- [ ] 5min spin
- [ ] binge watch VD
- [ ] Painting.

Health & wellbeing

Hours of sleep
Sleep tracker: 😴 😴 😴 😴 😴 😴   ○ ○ ○
         1 2 3 4 5 6 7 8 9 10

Exercise
Time: 15 min
Activity: mutipul

Today's Water intake
🥛🥛🥛🥛🥛🥛🥛
Shade in

MEALS
- **B**:
- **L**: 4 digestives
- **D**: Pot noodle.

MY ACHIEVEMENTS TODAY

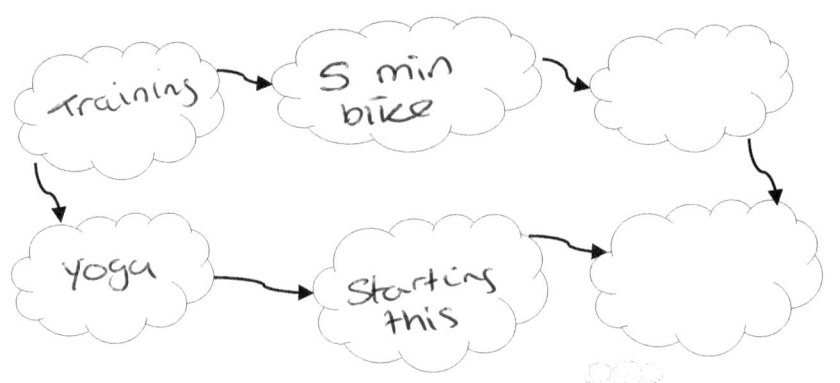

- training
- 5 min bike
- yoga
- Starting this

🌙 EVENING REFLECTIONS

Stuck to my training
Reached out to zoe + mandie
didn't go back to 2 sugars.
ate biscuits guilt free.
laughed.
cryed.

RATE MY DAY: 🤍 🤍 ❤️ 🤍 🤍

Daily Wellness Journal

Date: 19/ 1 /20 22   Sun Mon Tue (Wed) Thu Fri Sat

GRATEFUL for: Greg making me lunch. getting a office car

Today I CHOOSE TO FEEL
Determind

Today's GOOD HABITS
Stayed positive

Things I do well
- [ ] laughing with G
- [ ]
- [ ]
- [ ]
- [ ]
- [ ]

Self-Care
- [ ] yoga
- [ ] got dressed
- [ ] Ritual.
- [ ]
- [ ]
- [ ]

Health & wellbeing

Sleep tracker: Hours of sleep — 6
1 2 3 4 5 6 7 8 9 10

Exercise
Time: 20 min

Activity: yoga

Today's Water intake
(1 glass shaded of 7)
Shade in

MEALS
- **B** coffee
- **L** scrambled egg on toast
- **D** ~~coffee~~

MY ACHIEVEMENTS TODAY

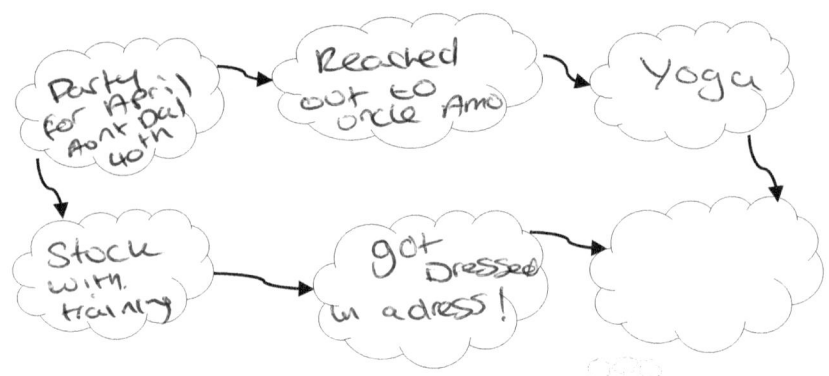

- Party for April Aont Del 40th
- Reached out to oncle Amo
- Yoga
- Stock with training
- Got dressed in a dress!

☾ EVENING REFLECTIONS

I've been a bit tense and snappy today. Maybe sitting doing training is taking its toll. Learning new things for work. Talking with G.

Slight spotting today + cramps may need to book an Dr app.

Laughed when found Shiya being chased by the flat faced cat.

Kid argueing

Shiya having a meltdown Wednesday. + Not wanting to do dodgeball any more

RATE MY DAY: ♥ ♥ ♥ ♥ ♥

Daily Wellness Journal

Date: 20 / 1 /20 22   Sun Mon Tue Wed Thu Fri Sat

GRATEFUL for: _____

Today I CHOOSE TO FEEL

Today's GOOD HABITS

Things I do well
- ☐ _____
- ☐ _____
- ☐ _____
- ☐ _____
- ☐ _____
- ☐ _____

Self-Care
- ☐ _____
- ☐ _____
- ☐ _____
- ☐ _____
- ☐ _____

Health & wellbeing

Sleep tracker: Hours of sleep ○ ○ ○ ○ ○ ○ ○ ○ ○ ○
1 2 3 4 5 6 7 8 9 10

Exercise
Time: _____

Activity: _____

Today's Water intake
🥛 🥛 🥛 🥛 🥛 🥛 🥛
Shade in

MEALS
B ....
L ....
D ....

MY ACHIEVEMENTS TODAY

EVENING REFLECTIONS

RATE MY DAY:

Daily Wellness Journal

Date: ___/___/20___   Sun   Mon   Tue   Wed   Thu   Fri   Sat

GRATEFUL for: _____

Today I CHOOSE TO FEEL

Today's GOOD HABITS

Things I do well
- [ ]
- [ ]
- [ ]
- [ ]
- [ ]
- [ ]

Self-Care
- [ ]
- [ ]
- [ ]
- [ ]
- [ ]
- [ ]

Health & wellbeing

Sleep tracker: Hours of sleep
○ ○ ○ ○ ○ ○ ○ ○ ○ ○
1 2 3 4 5 6 7 8 9 10

Exercise
Time: _____

Activity: _____

Today's Water intake
🥛 🥛 🥛 🥛 🥛 🥛 🥛
Shade in

MEALS
B ....
L ....
D ....

MY ACHIEVEMENTS TODAY

EVENING REFLECTIONS

RATE MY DAY:

Daily Wellness Journal

Date: ___/___/20___   Sun   Mon   Tue   Wed   Thu   Fri   Sat

GRATEFUL for: _____

Today I CHOOSE TO FEEL

Today's GOOD HABITS

Things I do well
- ☐ _____
- ☐ _____
- ☐ _____
- ☐ _____
- ☐ _____
- ☐ _____

Self-Care
- ☐ _____
- ☐ _____
- ☐ _____
- ☐ _____
- ☐ _____
- ☐ _____

Health & wellbeing

Sleep tracker: Hours of sleep
○ ○ ○ ○ ○ ○ ○ ○ ○ ○
1 2 3 4 5 6 7 8 9 10

Exercise
Time: _____

Activity: _____

Today's Water intake
🥛🥛🥛🥛🥛🥛🥛
Shade in

MEALS
B ···
L ···
D ···

MY ACHIEVEMENTS TODAY

☾ EVENING REFLECTIONS

RATE MY DAY:

Daily Wellness Journal

Date: ___/___/20___   Sun Mon Tue Wed Thu Fri Sat

GRATEFUL for: _____

Today I CHOOSE TO FEEL

Today's GOOD HABITS

Things I do well
- ☐ _____
- ☐ _____
- ☐ _____
- ☐ _____
- ☐ _____
- ☐ _____

Self-Care
- ☐ _____
- ☐ _____
- ☐ _____
- ☐ _____
- ☐ _____
- ☐ _____

Health & wellbeing

Sleep tracker: Hours of sleep
○ ○ ○ ○ ○ ○ ○ ○ ○ ○
1 2 3 4 5 6 7 8 9 10

Exercise
Time: _____

Activity: _____

Today's Water intake
🥛🥛🥛🥛🥛🥛🥛
Shade in

MEALS
B ....
L ....
D ....

MY ACHIEVEMENTS TODAY

EVENING REFLECTIONS

RATE MY DAY:

Daily Wellness Journal

Date: ___/___/20___   Sun Mon Tue Wed Thu Fri Sat

GRATEFUL for: _____

Today I CHOOSE TO FEEL

Today's GOOD HABITS

Things I do well
- ☐ _____
- ☐ _____
- ☐ _____
- ☐ _____
- ☐ _____
- ☐ _____

Self-Care
- ☐ _____
- ☐ _____
- ☐ _____
- ☐ _____
- ☐ _____
- ☐ _____

Health & wellbeing

Hours of sleep

Sleep tracker: ○ ○ ○ ○ ○ ○ ○ ○ ○ ○
                     1 2 3 4 5 6 7 8 9 10

Exercise
Time: _____

Activity: _____

Today's Water intake
⊔ ⊔ ⊔ ⊔ ⊔ ⊔ ⊔

Shade in

MEALS
B ....
L ....
D ....

MY ACHIEVEMENTS TODAY

EVENING REFLECTIONS

RATE MY DAY:

Daily Wellness Journal

Date: ___/___/20___   Sun   Mon   Tue   Wed   Thu   Fri   Sat

GRATEFUL for: _____

Today I CHOOSE TO FEEL

Today's GOOD HABITS

Things I do well
- ☐ _____
- ☐ _____
- ☐ _____
- ☐ _____
- ☐ _____
- ☐ _____

Self-Care
- ☐ _____
- ☐ _____
- ☐ _____
- ☐ _____
- ☐ _____
- ☐ _____

Health & wellbeing

Sleep tracker: Hours of sleep   1   2   3   4   5   6   7   8   9   10

Exercise
Time: _____

Activity: _____

Today's Water intake
Shade in

MEALS
- **B** ....
- **L** ....
- **D** ....

MY ACHIEVEMENTS TODAY

EVENING REFLECTIONS

RATE MY DAY:

Daily Wellness Journal

Date: ___/___/20___   Sun Mon Tue Wed Thu Fri Sat

GRATEFUL for: _____

Today I CHOOSE TO FEEL

Today's GOOD HABITS

Things I do well
- ☐ _____
- ☐ _____
- ☐ _____
- ☐ _____
- ☐ _____
- ☐ _____

Self-Care
- ☐ _____
- ☐ _____
- ☐ _____
- ☐ _____
- ☐ _____
- ☐ _____

Health & wellbeing

Sleep tracker: Hours of sleep
○ ○ ○ ○ ○ ○ ○ ○ ○ ○
1 2 3 4 5 6 7 8 9 10

Exercise
Time: _____

Activity: _____

Today's Water intake
🥛🥛🥛🥛🥛🥛🥛
Shade in

MEALS
B ....
L ....
D ....

MY ACHIEVEMENTS TODAY

EVENING REFLECTIONS

RATE MY DAY:

Daily Wellness Journal

Date: ___/___/20___   Sun Mon Tue Wed Thu Fri Sat

GRATEFUL for: _____

Today I CHOOSE TO FEEL

Today's GOOD HABITS

Things I do well
- ☐ _____
- ☐ _____
- ☐ _____
- ☐ _____
- ☐ _____
- ☐ _____

Self-Care
- ☐ _____
- ☐ _____
- ☐ _____
- ☐ _____
- ☐ _____
- ☐ _____

Health & wellbeing

Sleep tracker: Hours of sleep
○ ○ ○ ○ ○ ○ ○ ○ ○ ○
1 2 3 4 5 6 7 8 9 10

Exercise
Time: _____

Activity: _____

Today's Water intake
▽ ▽ ▽ ▽ ▽ ▽ ▽
Shade in

MEALS
B ....
L ....
D ....

MY ACHIEVEMENTS TODAY

☾ EVENING REFLECTIONS

RATE MY DAY:

Daily Wellness Journal

Date: ___/___/20___   Sun   Mon   Tue   Wed   Thu   Fri   Sat

GRATEFUL for: _____

Today I CHOOSE TO FEEL

Today's GOOD HABITS

Things I do well
- ☐ _____
- ☐ _____
- ☐ _____
- ☐ _____
- ☐ _____
- ☐ _____

Self-Care
- ☐ _____
- ☐ _____
- ☐ _____
- ☐ _____
- ☐ _____

Health & wellbeing

Sleep tracker: Hours of sleep
○ ○ ○ ○ ○ ○ ○ ○ ○ ○
1 2 3 4 5 6 7 8 9 10

Exercise
Time: _____

Activity: _____

Today's Water intake
🥛🥛🥛🥛🥛🥛🥛
Shade in

MEALS
- **B** ....
- **L** ....
- **D** ....

MY ACHIEVEMENTS TODAY

EVENING REFLECTIONS

RATE MY DAY:

Daily Wellness Journal

Date: ___/___/20___   Sun Mon Tue Wed Thu Fri Sat

GRATEFUL for: _____

Today I CHOOSE TO FEEL

Today's GOOD HABITS

Things I do well
- ☐ _____
- ☐ _____
- ☐ _____
- ☐ _____
- ☐ _____
- ☐ _____

Self-Care
- ☐ _____
- ☐ _____
- ☐ _____
- ☐ _____
- ☐ _____
- ☐ _____

Health & wellbeing

Sleep tracker: Hours of sleep ○ ○ ○ ○ ○ ○ ○ ○ ○ ○
1 2 3 4 5 6 7 8 9 10

Exercise
Time: _____

Activity: _____

Today's Water intake
🥤🥤🥤🥤🥤🥤🥤
Shade in

MEALS
- **B** ....
- **L** ....
- **D** ....

MY ACHIEVEMENTS TODAY

☾ EVENING REFLECTIONS

RATE MY DAY:

Daily Wellness Journal

Date: ___/___/20___   Sun Mon Tue Wed Thu Fri Sat

GRATEFUL for: _____

Today I CHOOSE TO FEEL

Today's GOOD HABITS

Things I do well
- ☐ _____
- ☐ _____
- ☐ _____
- ☐ _____
- ☐ _____
- ☐ _____

Self-Care
- ☐ _____
- ☐ _____
- ☐ _____
- ☐ _____
- ☐ _____
- ☐ _____

Health & wellbeing

Hours of sleep

Sleep tracker: ○ ○ ○ ○ ○ ○ ○ ○ ○ ○
                    1 2 3 4 5 6 7 8 9 10

Exercise
Time: _____

Activity: _____

Today's Water intake
[glass][glass][glass][glass][glass][glass][glass]

Shade in

MEALS
- **B** ....
- **L** ....
- **D** ....

MY ACHIEVEMENTS TODAY

☾ EVENING REFLECTIONS

RATE MY DAY:

Daily Wellness Journal

Date: ___/___/20___   Sun Mon Tue Wed Thu Fri Sat

GRATEFUL for: _____

Today I CHOOSE TO FEEL

Today's GOOD HABITS

Things I do well
- ☐ _____
- ☐ _____
- ☐ _____
- ☐ _____
- ☐ _____
- ☐ _____

Self-Care
- ☐ _____
- ☐ _____
- ☐ _____
- ☐ _____
- ☐ _____
- ☐ _____

Health & wellbeing

Hours of sleep

Sleep tracker: ○ ○ ○ ○ ○ ○ ○ ○ ○ ○
                    1 2 3 4 5 6 7 8 9 10

Exercise
Time: _____

Activity: _____

Today's Water intake
🥛🥛🥛🥛🥛🥛🥛
Shade in

MEALS
B ....
L ....
D ....

MY ACHIEVEMENTS TODAY

☾ EVENING REFLECTIONS

RATE MY DAY:

Daily Wellness Journal

Date: ___/___/20___   Sun Mon Tue Wed Thu Fri Sat

GRATEFUL for: _____

Today I CHOOSE TO FEEL

Today's GOOD HABITS

Things I do well
- ☐ _____
- ☐ _____
- ☐ _____
- ☐ _____
- ☐ _____
- ☐ _____

Self-Care
- ☐ _____
- ☐ _____
- ☐ _____
- ☐ _____
- ☐ _____
- ☐ _____

Health & wellbeing

Sleep tracker: Hours of sleep ○ ○ ○ ○ ○ ○ ○ ○ ○ ○
                                1 2 3 4 5 6 7 8 9 10

Exercise
Time: _____

Activity: _____

Today's Water intake
🥛🥛🥛🥛🥛🥛🥛🥛

Shade in

MEALS
B ....
L ....
D ....

MY ACHIEVEMENTS TODAY

EVENING REFLECTIONS

RATE MY DAY:

Daily Wellness Journal

Date: ___/___/20___   Sun Mon Tue Wed Thu Fri Sat

GRATEFUL for: _____

Today I CHOOSE TO FEEL

Today's GOOD HABITS

Things I do well
- ☐ _____
- ☐ _____
- ☐ _____
- ☐ _____
- ☐ _____
- ☐ _____

Self-Care
- ☐ _____
- ☐ _____
- ☐ _____
- ☐ _____
- ☐ _____
- ☐ _____

Health & wellbeing

Sleep tracker: Hours of sleep
○ ○ ○ ○ ○ ○ ○ ○ ○ ○
1 2 3 4 5 6 7 8 9 10

Exercise
Time: _____

Activity: _____

Today's Water intake
🥛🥛🥛🥛🥛🥛🥛
Shade in

MEALS
B ....
L ....
D ....

MY ACHIEVEMENTS TODAY

EVENING REFLECTIONS

RATE MY DAY:

Daily Wellness Journal

Date: ___/___/20___   Sun Mon Tue Wed Thu Fri Sat

GRATEFUL for: _____

Today I CHOOSE TO FEEL

Today's GOOD HABITS

Things I do well
- ☐ _____
- ☐ _____
- ☐ _____
- ☐ _____
- ☐ _____
- ☐ _____

Self-Care
- ☐ _____
- ☐ _____
- ☐ _____
- ☐ _____
- ☐ _____
- ☐ _____

Health & wellbeing

Hours of sleep

Sleep tracker: ○ ○ ○ ○ ○ ○ ○ ○ ○ ○
               1 2 3 4 5 6 7 8 9 10

Exercise
Time: _____

Activity: _____

Today's Water intake
🥛🥛🥛🥛🥛🥛🥛🥛

Shade in

MEALS

B ···
L ···
D ···

MY ACHIEVEMENTS TODAY

☾ EVENING REFLECTIONS

RATE MY DAY:

Daily Wellness Journal

Date: ___/___/20___   Sun Mon Tue Wed Thu Fri Sat

GRATEFUL for: _____

Today I CHOOSE TO FEEL

Today's GOOD HABITS

Things I do well
- [ ] _____
- [ ] _____
- [ ] _____
- [ ] _____
- [ ] _____
- [ ] _____

Self-Care
- [ ] _____
- [ ] _____
- [ ] _____
- [ ] _____
- [ ] _____
- [ ] _____

Health & wellbeing

Sleep tracker: Hours of sleep
1 2 3 4 5 6 7 8 9 10

Exercise
Time: _____

Activity: _____

Today's Water intake
Shade in

MEALS
B ....
L ....
D ....

MY ACHIEVEMENTS TODAY

☾ EVENING REFLECTIONS

RATE MY DAY:

Daily Wellness Journal

Date: ___/___/20___   Sun Mon Tue Wed Thu Fri Sat

GRATEFUL for: _____

Today I CHOOSE TO FEEL

Today's GOOD HABITS

Things I do well
- ☐ _____
- ☐ _____
- ☐ _____
- ☐ _____
- ☐ _____
- ☐ _____

Self-Care
- ☐ _____
- ☐ _____
- ☐ _____
- ☐ _____
- ☐ _____
- ☐ _____

Health & wellbeing

Hours of sleep

Sleep tracker: ○ ○ ○ ○ ○ ○ ○ ○ ○ ○
                              1 2 3 4 5 6 7 8 9 10

Exercise
Time: _____

Activity: _____

Today's Water intake
🥛🥛🥛🥛🥛🥛🥛

Shade in

MEALS

B ···

L ···

D ···

MY ACHIEVEMENTS TODAY

☪ EVENING REFLECTIONS

RATE MY DAY:

Daily Wellness Journal

Date: ___/___/20___   Sun Mon Tue Wed Thu Fri Sat

GRATEFUL for: _____

Today I CHOOSE TO FEEL

Today's GOOD HABITS

Things I do well
- ☐ _____
- ☐ _____
- ☐ _____
- ☐ _____
- ☐ _____
- ☐ _____

Self-Care
- ☐ _____
- ☐ _____
- ☐ _____
- ☐ _____
- ☐ _____
- ☐ _____
- ☐ _____

Health & wellbeing

Sleep tracker: Hours of sleep
○ ○ ○ ○ ○ ○ ○ ○ ○ ○
1 2 3 4 5 6 7 8 9 10

Exercise
Time: _____

Activity: _____

Today's Water intake
🥛 🥛 🥛 🥛 🥛 🥛 🥛
Shade in

MEALS
B ....
L ....
D ....

MY ACHIEVEMENTS TODAY

☪ EVENING REFLECTIONS

RATE MY DAY:

Daily Wellness Journal

Date: ___/___/20___   Sun Mon Tue Wed Thu Fri Sat

GRATEFUL for: _____

Today I CHOOSE TO FEEL

Today's GOOD HABITS

Things I do well
- ☐ _____
- ☐ _____
- ☐ _____
- ☐ _____
- ☐ _____
- ☐ _____

Self-Care
- ☐ _____
- ☐ _____
- ☐ _____
- ☐ _____
- ☐ _____
- ☐ _____

Health & wellbeing

Sleep tracker: Hours of sleep
○ ○ ○ ○ ○ ○ ○ ○ ○ ○
1 2 3 4 5 6 7 8 9 10

Exercise
Time: _____
Activity: _____

Today's Water intake
▽▽▽▽▽▽▽
Shade in

MEALS
B ....
L ....
D ....

MY ACHIEVEMENTS TODAY

EVENING REFLECTIONS

RATE MY DAY:

Daily Wellness Journal

Date: ___/___/20___   Sun   Mon   Tue   Wed   Thu   Fri   Sat

GRATEFUL for: _____

Today I CHOOSE TO FEEL

Today's GOOD HABITS

Things I do well
- [ ] _____
- [ ] _____
- [ ] _____
- [ ] _____
- [ ] _____
- [ ] _____

Self-Care
- [ ] _____
- [ ] _____
- [ ] _____
- [ ] _____
- [ ] _____
- [ ] _____

Health & wellbeing

Sleep tracker: Hours of sleep
○ ○ ○ ○ ○ ○ ○ ○ ○ ○
1 2 3 4 5 6 7 8 9 10

Exercise
Time: _____

Activity: _____

Today's Water intake
🥛 🥛 🥛 🥛 🥛 🥛 🥛
Shade in

MEALS
B ....
L ....
D ....

MY ACHIEVEMENTS TODAY

☾ EVENING REFLECTIONS

RATE MY DAY:

Daily Wellness Journal

Date: ___/___/20___   Sun   Mon   Tue   Wed   Thu   Fri   Sat

GRATEFUL for: _____

Today I CHOOSE TO FEEL

Today's GOOD HABITS

Things I do well
- ☐ _____
- ☐ _____
- ☐ _____
- ☐ _____
- ☐ _____
- ☐ _____

Self-Care
- ☐ _____
- ☐ _____
- ☐ _____
- ☐ _____
- ☐ _____
- ☐ _____

Health & wellbeing

Hours of sleep

Sleep tracker: ○ ○ ○ ○ ○ ○ ○ ○ ○ ○
                1 2 3 4 5 6 7 8 9 10

Exercise
Time: _____

Activity: _____

Today's Water intake

Shade in

MEALS

B ....

L ....

D ....

MY ACHIEVEMENTS TODAY

☾ EVENING REFLECTIONS

RATE MY DAY:

health is wealth

Daily Wellness Journal

Date: ___/___/20___   Sun Mon Tue Wed Thu Fri Sat

GRATEFUL for: _____
_____

Today I CHOOSE TO FEEL
_____
_____
_____

Today's GOOD HABITS
_____
_____
_____

Things I do well
- ☐ _____
- ☐ _____
- ☐ _____
- ☐ _____
- ☐ _____
- ☐ _____

Self-Care
- ☐ _____
- ☐ _____
- ☐ _____
- ☐ _____
- ☐ _____
- ☐ _____

Health & wellbeing

Sleep tracker: Hours of sleep
○ ○ ○ ○ ○ ○ ○ ○ ○ ○
1 2 3 4 5 6 7 8 9 10

Exercise
Time: _____

Activity: _____

Today's Water intake
🥛 🥛 🥛 🥛 🥛 🥛 🥛 🥛
Shade in

MEALS
B ....
L ....
D ....

MY ACHIEVEMENTS TODAY

EVENING REFLECTIONS

RATE MY DAY:

Daily Wellness Journal

Date: ___/___/20___   Sun Mon Tue Wed Thu Fri Sat

GRATEFUL for: _____
_____

Today I CHOOSE TO FEEL

Today's GOOD HABITS

Things I do well
- ☐ _____
- ☐ _____
- ☐ _____
- ☐ _____
- ☐ _____
- ☐ _____

Self-Care
- ☐ _____
- ☐ _____
- ☐ _____
- ☐ _____
- ☐ _____
- ☐ _____

Health & wellbeing

Sleep tracker: Hours of sleep
◯ ◯ ◯ ◯ ◯ ◯ ◯ ◯ ◯ ◯
1 2 3 4 5 6 7 8 9 10

Exercise
Time: _____

Activity: _____

Today's Water intake
🥛🥛🥛🥛🥛🥛🥛🥛
Shade in

MEALS
B ....
L ....
D ....

MY ACHIEVEMENTS TODAY

☾ EVENING REFLECTIONS

RATE MY DAY:

Daily Wellness Journal

Date: ___/___/20___   Sun Mon Tue Wed Thu Fri Sat

GRATEFUL for: _____

Today I CHOOSE TO FEEL

Today's GOOD HABITS

Things I do well
- ☐ _____
- ☐ _____
- ☐ _____
- ☐ _____
- ☐ _____
- ☐ _____

Self-Care
- ☐ _____
- ☐ _____
- ☐ _____
- ☐ _____
- ☐ _____
- ☐ _____

Health & wellbeing

Sleep tracker: Hours of sleep
○ ○ ○ ○ ○ ○ ○ ○ ○ ○
1 2 3 4 5 6 7 8 9 10

Exercise
Time: _____

Activity: _____

Today's Water intake
🥛 🥛 🥛 🥛 🥛 🥛 🥛 🥛
Shade in

MEALS
B ··
L ··
D ··

MY ACHIEVEMENTS TODAY

EVENING REFLECTIONS

RATE MY DAY:

Daily Wellness Journal

Date: ___/___/20___   Sun Mon Tue Wed Thu Fri Sat

GRATEFUL for: _____

Today I CHOOSE TO FEEL

Today's GOOD HABITS

Things I do well
- ☐ _____
- ☐ _____
- ☐ _____
- ☐ _____
- ☐ _____
- ☐ _____

Self-Care
- ☐ _____
- ☐ _____
- ☐ _____
- ☐ _____
- ☐ _____
- ☐ _____

Health & wellbeing

Sleep tracker: Hours of sleep 1 2 3 4 5 6 7 8 9 10

Exercise
Time: _____
Activity: _____

Today's Water intake
Shade in

MEALS
- **B** ....
- **L** ....
- **D** ....

MY ACHIEVEMENTS TODAY

☾ EVENING REFLECTIONS

RATE MY DAY:

Daily Wellness Journal

Date: ___/___/20___   Sun Mon Tue Wed Thu Fri Sat

GRATEFUL for: _____

Today I CHOOSE TO FEEL

Today's GOOD HABITS

Things I do well
- ☐ _____
- ☐ _____
- ☐ _____
- ☐ _____
- ☐ _____
- ☐ _____

Self-Care
- ☐ _____
- ☐ _____
- ☐ _____
- ☐ _____
- ☐ _____
- ☐ _____

Health & wellbeing

Sleep tracker: Hours of sleep
○ ○ ○ ○ ○ ○ ○ ○ ○ ○
1 2 3 4 5 6 7 8 9 10

Exercise
Time: _____

Activity: _____

Today's Water intake
🥛 🥛 🥛 🥛 🥛 🥛 🥛 🥛
Shade in

MEALS

B ....

L ....

D ....

MY ACHIEVEMENTS TODAY

☪ EVENING REFLECTIONS

RATE MY DAY:

Daily Wellness Journal

Date: ___/___/20___   Sun Mon Tue Wed Thu Fri Sat

GRATEFUL for: _____

Today I CHOOSE TO FEEL

Today's GOOD HABITS

Things I do well
- ☐ _____
- ☐ _____
- ☐ _____
- ☐ _____
- ☐ _____
- ☐ _____

Self-Care
- ☐ _____
- ☐ _____
- ☐ _____
- ☐ _____
- ☐ _____
- ☐ _____

Health & wellbeing

Sleep tracker: Hours of sleep
○ ○ ○ ○ ○ ○ ○ ○ ○ ○
1 2 3 4 5 6 7 8 9 10

Exercise
Time: _____

Activity: _____

Today's Water intake
🥛 🥛 🥛 🥛 🥛 🥛 🥛 🥛

Shade in

MEALS

B ....

L ....

D ....

MY ACHIEVEMENTS TODAY

EVENING REFLECTIONS

RATE MY DAY:

Daily Wellness Journal

Date: ___/___/20___   Sun Mon Tue Wed Thu Fri Sat

GRATEFUL for: _____

_____

Today I CHOOSE TO FEEL

Today's GOOD HABITS

Things I do well

- [ ]
- [ ]
- [ ]
- [ ]
- [ ]
- [ ]

Self-Care

- [ ]
- [ ]
- [ ]
- [ ]
- [ ]
- [ ]

Health & wellbeing

Sleep tracker: Hours of sleep
1 2 3 4 5 6 7 8 9 10

Exercise

Time: _____

Activity: _____

Today's Water intake

Shade in

MEALS

B ....

L ....

D ....

MY ACHIEVEMENTS TODAY

EVENING REFLECTIONS

RATE MY DAY:

Daily Wellness Journal

Date: ___/___/20___   Sun Mon Tue Wed Thu Fri Sat

GRATEFUL for: _____
_____

Today I CHOOSE TO FEEL
_____
_____
_____

Today's GOOD HABITS
_____
_____
_____

Things I do well
- [ ] _____
- [ ] _____
- [ ] _____
- [ ] _____
- [ ] _____
- [ ] _____

Self-Care
- [ ] _____
- [ ] _____
- [ ] _____
- [ ] _____
- [ ] _____
- [ ] _____

Health & wellbeing

Sleep tracker: Hours of sleep
○ ○ ○ ○ ○ ○ ○ ○ ○ ○
1 2 3 4 5 6 7 8 9 10

Exercise
Time: _____
Activity: _____

Today's Water intake
▽ ▽ ▽ ▽ ▽ ▽ ▽
Shade in

MEALS
B ....
L ....
D ....

MY ACHIEVEMENTS TODAY

EVENING REFLECTIONS

RATE MY DAY:

Daily Wellness Journal

Date: ___/___/20___   Sun Mon Tue Wed Thu Fri Sat

GRATEFUL for: _____

Today I CHOOSE TO FEEL

Today's GOOD HABITS

Things I do well
- ☐ _____
- ☐ _____
- ☐ _____
- ☐ _____
- ☐ _____
- ☐ _____

Self-Care
- ☐ _____
- ☐ _____
- ☐ _____
- ☐ _____
- ☐ _____
- ☐ _____

Health & wellbeing

Sleep tracker: Hours of sleep
○ ○ ○ ○ ○ ○ ○ ○ ○ ○
1 2 3 4 5 6 7 8 9 10

Exercise
Time: _____

Activity: _____

Today's Water intake
🥛 🥛 🥛 🥛 🥛 🥛 🥛 🥛

Shade in

MEALS

B ....

L ....

D ....

MY ACHIEVEMENTS TODAY

EVENING REFLECTIONS

_____
_____
_____
_____
_____
_____
_____
_____
_____
_____
_____
_____
_____
_____
_____
_____
_____
_____

RATE MY DAY:

Daily Wellness Journal

Date: ___/___/20___   Sun   Mon   Tue   Wed   Thu   Fri   Sat

GRATEFUL for: _____
_____

Today I CHOOSE TO FEEL

Today's GOOD HABITS

Things I do well

- ☐ _____
- ☐ _____
- ☐ _____
- ☐ _____
- ☐ _____
- ☐ _____

Self-Care

- ☐ _____
- ☐ _____
- ☐ _____
- ☐ _____
- ☐ _____
- ☐ _____

Health & wellbeing

Hours of sleep
Sleep tracker: ○ ○ ○ ○ ○ ○ ○ ○ ○ ○
              1 2 3 4 5 6 7 8 9 10

Exercise
Time: _____

Activity: _____

Today's Water intake

Shade in

MEALS

B ....
L ....
D ....

MY ACHIEVEMENTS TODAY

EVENING REFLECTIONS

RATE MY DAY:

Daily Wellness Journal

Date: ___/___/20___   Sun   Mon   Tue   Wed   Thu   Fri   Sat

GRATEFUL for: _____
_____

Today I CHOOSE TO FEEL

Today's GOOD HABITS

Things I do well
- ☐ _____
- ☐ _____
- ☐ _____
- ☐ _____
- ☐ _____
- ☐ _____

Self-Care
- ☐ _____
- ☐ _____
- ☐ _____
- ☐ _____
- ☐ _____
- ☐ _____

Health & wellbeing

Sleep tracker: Hours of sleep
○ ○ ○ ○ ○ ○ ○ ○ ○ ○
1   2   3   4   5   6   7   8   9   10

Exercise
Time: _____

Activity: _____

Today's Water intake
🥛 🥛 🥛 🥛 🥛 🥛 🥛 🥛
Shade in

MEALS
B ....
L ....
D ....

MY ACHIEVEMENTS TODAY

EVENING REFLECTIONS

RATE MY DAY:

Daily Wellness Journal

Date: ___/___/20___   Sun Mon Tue Wed Thu Fri Sat

GRATEFUL for: _____

Today I CHOOSE TO FEEL

Today's GOOD HABITS

Things I do well
- ☐ _____
- ☐ _____
- ☐ _____
- ☐ _____
- ☐ _____
- ☐ _____

Self-Care
- ☐ _____
- ☐ _____
- ☐ _____
- ☐ _____
- ☐ _____
- ☐ _____

Health & wellbeing

Sleep tracker: Hours of sleep
○ ○ ○ ○ ○ ○ ○ ○ ○ ○
1 2 3 4 5 6 7 8 9 10

Exercise
Time: _____

Activity: _____

Today's Water intake
🥛🥛🥛🥛🥛🥛🥛🥛
Shade in

MEALS
B ....
L ....
D ....

MY ACHIEVEMENTS TODAY

EVENING REFLECTIONS

RATE MY DAY:

Daily Wellness Journal

Date: ___/___/20___   Sun   Mon   Tue   Wed   Thu   Fri   Sat

GRATEFUL for: _____

Today I CHOOSE TO FEEL

Today's GOOD HABITS

Things I do well
- [ ] _____
- [ ] _____
- [ ] _____
- [ ] _____
- [ ] _____
- [ ] _____

Self-Care
- [ ] _____
- [ ] _____
- [ ] _____
- [ ] _____
- [ ] _____
- [ ] _____

Health & wellbeing

Sleep tracker: Hours of sleep ◯ ◯ ◯ ◯ ◯ ◯ ◯ ◯ ◯ ◯
                                1 2 3 4 5 6 7 8 9 10

Exercise
Time: _____
Activity: _____

Today's Water intake
🥛 🥛 🥛 🥛 🥛 🥛 🥛 🥛
Shade in

MEALS
B ....
L ....
D ....

MY ACHIEVEMENTS TODAY

EVENING REFLECTIONS

RATE MY DAY:

Daily Wellness Journal

Date: ___/___/20___   Sun   Mon   Tue   Wed   Thu   Fri   Sat

GRATEFUL for: _____

Today I CHOOSE TO FEEL

Today's GOOD HABITS

Things I do well

- [ ]
- [ ]
- [ ]
- [ ]
- [ ]
- [ ]

Self-Care

- [ ]
- [ ]
- [ ]
- [ ]
- [ ]
- [ ]

Health & wellbeing

Sleep tracker: ○ ○ ○ ○ ○ ○ ○ ○ ○ ○
Hours of sleep
1 2 3 4 5 6 7 8 9 10

Exercise
Time: _____

Activity: _____

Today's Water intake
🥛🥛🥛🥛🥛🥛🥛🥛
Shade in

MEALS
B ....
L ....
D ....

MY ACHIEVEMENTS TODAY

EVENING REFLECTIONS

RATE MY DAY:

Daily Wellness Journal

Date: ___/___/20___   Sun   Mon   Tue   Wed   Thu   Fri   Sat

GRATEFUL for: _____

Today I CHOOSE TO FEEL

Today's GOOD HABITS

Things I do well
- ☐ _____
- ☐ _____
- ☐ _____
- ☐ _____
- ☐ _____
- ☐ _____

Self-Care
- ☐ _____
- ☐ _____
- ☐ _____
- ☐ _____
- ☐ _____
- ☐ _____

Health & wellbeing

Sleep tracker: Hours of sleep   ○ ○ ○ ○ ○ ○ ○ ○ ○ ○
                                  1 2 3 4 5 6 7 8 9 10

Exercise
Time: _____

Activity: _____

Today's Water intake
🥛 🥛 🥛 🥛 🥛 🥛 🥛
Shade in

MEALS
B ....
L ....
D ....

MY ACHIEVEMENTS TODAY

☾ EVENING REFLECTIONS

_____

RATE MY DAY:

Daily Wellness Journal

Date: ___/___/20___   Sun Mon Tue Wed Thu Fri Sat

GRATEFUL for: _____

Today I CHOOSE TO FEEL

Today's GOOD HABITS

Things I do well
- ☐
- ☐
- ☐
- ☐
- ☐
- ☐

Self-Care
- ☐
- ☐
- ☐
- ☐
- ☐
- ☐

Health & wellbeing

Hours of sleep
Sleep tracker: ◯ ◯ ◯ ◯ ◯ ◯ ◯ ◯ ◯ ◯
          1 2 3 4 5 6 7 8 9 10

Exercise
Time: _____

Activity: _____

Today's Water intake
🥛🥛🥛🥛🥛🥛🥛
Shade in

MEALS
B ....
L ....
D ....

MY ACHIEVEMENTS TODAY

EVENING REFLECTIONS

RATE MY DAY:

Daily Wellness Journal

Date: ___/___/20___   Sun   Mon   Tue   Wed   Thu   Fri   Sat

GRATEFUL for: _____

Today I CHOOSE TO FEEL

Today's GOOD HABITS

Things I do well
- ☐ _____
- ☐ _____
- ☐ _____
- ☐ _____
- ☐ _____
- ☐ _____

Self-Care
- ☐ _____
- ☐ _____
- ☐ _____
- ☐ _____
- ☐ _____
- ☐ _____

Health & wellbeing

Sleep tracker: Hours of sleep
○ ○ ○ ○ ○ ○ ○ ○ ○ ○
1 2 3 4 5 6 7 8 9 10

Exercise
Time: _____

Activity: _____

Today's Water intake
🥛 🥛 🥛 🥛 🥛 🥛 🥛 🥛
Shade in

MEALS

B ....

L ....

D ....

MY ACHIEVEMENTS TODAY

EVENING REFLECTIONS

RATE MY DAY:

To Plant A GARDEN *is to believe* IN TOMORROW

Daily Wellness Journal

Date: ___/___/20___   Sun Mon Tue Wed Thu Fri Sat

GRATEFUL for: _____
_____

Today I CHOOSE TO FEEL

Today's GOOD HABITS

Things I do well
- ☐ _____
- ☐ _____
- ☐ _____
- ☐ _____
- ☐ _____
- ☐ _____

Self-Care
- ☐ _____
- ☐ _____
- ☐ _____
- ☐ _____
- ☐ _____
- ☐ _____

Health & wellbeing

Hours of sleep
Sleep tracker: ◯ ◯ ◯ ◯ ◯ ◯ ◯ ◯ ◯ ◯
1 2 3 4 5 6 7 8 9 10

Exercise
Time: _____

Activity: _____

Today's Water intake
🥛🥛🥛🥛🥛🥛🥛
Shade in

MEALS
B ....
L ....
D ....

MY ACHIEVEMENTS TODAY

EVENING REFLECTIONS

RATE MY DAY:

Daily Wellness Journal

Date: ___/___/20___   Sun   Mon   Tue   Wed   Thu   Fri   Sat

GRATEFUL for: _____

Today I CHOOSE TO FEEL

Today's GOOD HABITS

Things I do well
- ☐ _____
- ☐ _____
- ☐ _____
- ☐ _____
- ☐ _____
- ☐ _____

Self-Care
- ☐ _____
- ☐ _____
- ☐ _____
- ☐ _____
- ☐ _____
- ☐ _____

Health & wellbeing

Hours of sleep

Sleep tracker: ○ ○ ○ ○ ○ ○ ○ ○ ○ ○
                       1 2 3 4 5 6 7 8 9 10

Exercise
Time: _____

Activity: _____

Today's Water intake

🥛 🥛 🥛 🥛 🥛 🥛 🥛

Shade in

MEALS

B ....

L ....

D ....

MY ACHIEVEMENTS TODAY

EVENING REFLECTIONS

RATE MY DAY:

Daily Wellness Journal

Date: ___/___/20___   Sun Mon Tue Wed Thu Fri Sat

GRATEFUL for: _____

Today I CHOOSE TO FEEL

Today's GOOD HABITS

Things I do well
- [ ]
- [ ]
- [ ]
- [ ]
- [ ]
- [ ]

Self-Care
- [ ]
- [ ]
- [ ]
- [ ]
- [ ]
- [ ]

Health & wellbeing

Sleep tracker: Hours of sleep
1 2 3 4 5 6 7 8 9 10

Exercise
Time: _____

Activity: _____

Today's Water intake
🥤🥤🥤🥤🥤🥤🥤
Shade in

MEALS
B ....
L ....
D ....

MY ACHIEVEMENTS TODAY

☾ EVENING REFLECTIONS

RATE MY DAY:

Daily Wellness Journal

Date: ___/___/20___   Sun Mon Tue Wed Thu Fri Sat

GRATEFUL for: _____

Today I CHOOSE TO FEEL

Today's GOOD HABITS

Things I do well
- ☐ _____
- ☐ _____
- ☐ _____
- ☐ _____
- ☐ _____
- ☐ _____

Self-Care
- ☐ _____
- ☐ _____
- ☐ _____
- ☐ _____
- ☐ _____
- ☐ _____

Health & wellbeing

Sleep tracker: Hours of sleep ○ ○ ○ ○ ○ ○ ○ ○ ○ ○
                                1 2 3 4 5 6 7 8 9 10

Exercise
Time: _____

Activity: _____

Today's Water intake
🥛🥛🥛🥛🥛🥛🥛
Shade in

MEALS
B ··
L ··
D ··

MY ACHIEVEMENTS TODAY

☾ EVENING REFLECTIONS

RATE MY DAY:

Daily Wellness Journal

Date: ___/___/20___   Sun Mon Tue Wed Thu Fri Sat

GRATEFUL for: _____
_____

Today I CHOOSE TO FEEL

Today's GOOD HABITS

Things I do well
- ☐ _____
- ☐ _____
- ☐ _____
- ☐ _____
- ☐ _____
- ☐ _____

Self-Care
- ☐ _____
- ☐ _____
- ☐ _____
- ☐ _____
- ☐ _____
- ☐ _____

Health & wellbeing

Sleep tracker: Hours of sleep
○ ○ ○ ○ ○ ○ ○ ○ ○ ○
1 2 3 4 5 6 7 8 9 10

Exercise
Time: _____

Activity: _____

Today's Water intake
🥛 🥛 🥛 🥛 🥛 🥛 🥛
Shade in

MEALS
B ....
L ....
D ....

MY ACHIEVEMENTS TODAY

☾ EVENING REFLECTIONS

RATE MY DAY:

Daily Wellness Journal

Date: ___/___/20___   Sun Mon Tue Wed Thu Fri Sat

GRATEFUL for: _____

Today I CHOOSE TO FEEL

Today's GOOD HABITS

Things I do well

- [ ] _____
- [ ] _____
- [ ] _____
- [ ] _____
- [ ] _____
- [ ] _____

Self-Care

- [ ] _____
- [ ] _____
- [ ] _____
- [ ] _____
- [ ] _____
- [ ] _____

Health & wellbeing

Sleep tracker: Hours of sleep
○ ○ ○ ○ ○ ○ ○ ○ ○ ○
1 2 3 4 5 6 7 8 9 10

Exercise
Time: _____
Activity: _____

Today's Water intake
⬜⬜⬜⬜⬜⬜⬜
Shade in

MEALS

B ....
L ....
D ....

MY ACHIEVEMENTS TODAY

EVENING REFLECTIONS

RATE MY DAY:

Daily Wellness Journal

Date: ___/___/20___   Sun   Mon   Tue   Wed   Thu   Fri   Sat

GRATEFUL for: _____

Today I CHOOSE TO FEEL

Today's GOOD HABITS

Things I do well
- ☐ _____
- ☐ _____
- ☐ _____
- ☐ _____
- ☐ _____
- ☐ _____

Self-Care
- ☐ _____
- ☐ _____
- ☐ _____
- ☐ _____
- ☐ _____
- ☐ _____

Health & wellbeing

Sleep tracker: Hours of sleep   1 2 3 4 5 6 7 8 9 10

Exercise
Time: _____
Activity: _____

Today's Water intake
Shade in

MEALS
B ....
L ....
D ....

MY ACHIEVEMENTS TODAY

☾ EVENING REFLECTIONS

RATE MY DAY:

Daily Wellness Journal

Date: ___/___/20___   Sun Mon Tue Wed Thu Fri Sat

GRATEFUL for: _____

Today I CHOOSE TO FEEL

Today's GOOD HABITS

Things I do well
- ☐ _____
- ☐ _____
- ☐ _____
- ☐ _____
- ☐ _____
- ☐ _____

Self-Care
- ☐ _____
- ☐ _____
- ☐ _____
- ☐ _____
- ☐ _____
- ☐ _____

Health & wellbeing

Sleep tracker: Hours of sleep
○ ○ ○ ○ ○ ○ ○ ○ ○ ○
1 2 3 4 5 6 7 8 9 10

Exercise
Time: _____

Activity: _____

Today's Water intake
🥛 🥛 🥛 🥛 🥛 🥛 🥛
Shade in

MEALS
B ....
L ....
D ....

MY ACHIEVEMENTS TODAY

EVENING REFLECTIONS

RATE MY DAY:

Daily Wellness Journal

Date: ___/___/20___   Sun Mon Tue Wed Thu Fri Sat

GRATEFUL for: _____
_____

Today I CHOOSE TO FEEL

Today's GOOD HABITS

Things I do well
- ☐ _____
- ☐ _____
- ☐ _____
- ☐ _____
- ☐ _____
- ☐ _____

Self-Care
- ☐ _____
- ☐ _____
- ☐ _____
- ☐ _____
- ☐ _____
- ☐ _____

Health & wellbeing

Hours of sleep
Sleep tracker: ◯ ◯ ◯ ◯ ◯ ◯ ◯ ◯ ◯ ◯
　　　　　　　　1 2 3 4 5 6 7 8 9 10

Exercise
Time: _____

Activity: _____

Today's Water intake
🥛 🥛 🥛 🥛 🥛 🥛 🥛
Shade in

MEALS
B ....
L ....
D ....

MY ACHIEVEMENTS TODAY

EVENING REFLECTIONS

RATE MY DAY:

Daily Wellness Journal

Date: ___/___/20___   Sun Mon Tue Wed Thu Fri Sat

GRATEFUL for: _____

Today I CHOOSE TO FEEL

Today's GOOD HABITS

Things I do well
- [ ]
- [ ]
- [ ]
- [ ]
- [ ]
- [ ]

Self-Care
- [ ]
- [ ]
- [ ]
- [ ]
- [ ]
- [ ]

Health & wellbeing

Sleep tracker: ○ ○ ○ ○ ○ ○ ○ ○ ○ ○
Hours of sleep: 1 2 3 4 5 6 7 8 9 10

Exercise
Time: _____

Activity: _____

Today's Water intake
🥛 🥛 🥛 🥛 🥛 🥛 🥛
Shade in

MEALS
B ....
L ....
D ....

MY ACHIEVEMENTS TODAY

EVENING REFLECTIONS

RATE MY DAY:

Daily Wellness Journal

Date: ___/___/20___   Sun   Mon   Tue   Wed   Thu   Fri   Sat

GRATEFUL for: _____

Today I CHOOSE TO FEEL

Today's GOOD HABITS

Things I do well

- ☐ _____
- ☐ _____
- ☐ _____
- ☐ _____
- ☐ _____
- ☐ _____

Self-Care

- ☐ _____
- ☐ _____
- ☐ _____
- ☐ _____
- ☐ _____
- ☐ _____

Health & wellbeing

Sleep tracker: Hours of sleep
○ ○ ○ ○ ○ ○ ○ ○ ○ ○
1　2　3　4　5　6　7　8　9　10

Exercise
Time: _____

Activity: _____

Today's Water intake
🥛 🥛 🥛 🥛 🥛 🥛 🥛
Shade in

MEALS

B ....
L ....
D ....

MY ACHIEVEMENTS TODAY

☾ EVENING REFLECTIONS

RATE MY DAY:

Daily Wellness Journal

Date: ___/___/20___   Sun   Mon   Tue   Wed   Thu   Fri   Sat

GRATEFUL for: _____

Today I CHOOSE TO FEEL

Today's GOOD HABITS

Things I do well
- [ ] _____
- [ ] _____
- [ ] _____
- [ ] _____
- [ ] _____
- [ ] _____

Self-Care
- [ ] _____
- [ ] _____
- [ ] _____
- [ ] _____
- [ ] _____
- [ ] _____

Health & wellbeing

Sleep tracker: Hours of sleep
○ ○ ○ ○ ○ ○ ○ ○ ○ ○
1 2 3 4 5 6 7 8 9 10

Exercise
Time: _____

Activity: _____

Today's Water intake
🥛🥛🥛🥛🥛🥛🥛
Shade in

MEALS
B ....
L ....
D ....

MY ACHIEVEMENTS TODAY

☾ EVENING REFLECTIONS

RATE MY DAY:

live with intention

Daily Wellness Journal

Date: ___/___/20___   Sun   Mon   Tue   Wed   Thu   Fri   Sat

GRATEFUL for: _____

Today I CHOOSE TO FEEL

Today's GOOD HABITS

Things I do well

- [ ]
- [ ]
- [ ]
- [ ]
- [ ]
- [ ]

Self-Care

- [ ]
- [ ]
- [ ]
- [ ]
- [ ]
- [ ]

Health & wellbeing

Sleep tracker: Hours of sleep — 1 2 3 4 5 6 7 8 9 10

Exercise
Time: _____

Activity: _____

Today's Water intake
🥛 🥛 🥛 🥛 🥛 🥛 🥛 🥛

Shade in

MEALS

B ....

L ....

D ....

MY ACHIEVEMENTS TODAY

EVENING REFLECTIONS

RATE MY DAY:

Daily Wellness Journal

Date: ___/___/20___   Sun Mon Tue Wed Thu Fri Sat

GRATEFUL for: _____

Today I CHOOSE TO FEEL

Today's GOOD HABITS

Things I do well
- ☐ _____
- ☐ _____
- ☐ _____
- ☐ _____
- ☐ _____
- ☐ _____

Self-Care
- ☐ _____
- ☐ _____
- ☐ _____
- ☐ _____
- ☐ _____
- ☐ _____

Health & wellbeing

Sleep tracker: Hours of sleep ○ ○ ○ ○ ○ ○ ○ ○ ○ ○
                                1 2 3 4 5 6 7 8 9 10

Exercise
Time: _____

Activity: _____

Today's Water intake
⛾ ⛾ ⛾ ⛾ ⛾ ⛾ ⛾
Shade in

MEALS
B ....
L ....
D ....

MY ACHIEVEMENTS TODAY

EVENING REFLECTIONS

RATE MY DAY:

Daily Wellness Journal

Date: ___/___/20___   Sun Mon Tue Wed Thu Fri Sat

GRATEFUL for: _____

Today I CHOOSE TO FEEL

Today's GOOD HABITS

Things I do well
- ☐ _____
- ☐ _____
- ☐ _____
- ☐ _____
- ☐ _____
- ☐ _____

Self-Care
- ☐ _____
- ☐ _____
- ☐ _____
- ☐ _____
- ☐ _____
- ☐ _____

Health & wellbeing

Sleep tracker: Hours of sleep
○ ○ ○ ○ ○ ○ ○ ○ ○ ○
1 2 3 4 5 6 7 8 9 10

Exercise
Time: _____

Activity: _____

Today's Water intake
🥛 🥛 🥛 🥛 🥛 🥛 🥛
Shade in

MEALS

B ....

L ....

D ....

MY ACHIEVEMENTS TODAY

☾ EVENING REFLECTIONS

RATE MY DAY:

Daily Wellness Journal

Date: ___/___/20___   Sun   Mon   Tue   Wed   Thu   Fri   Sat

GRATEFUL for: _____
_____

Today I CHOOSE TO FEEL

Today's GOOD HABITS

Things I do well
- ☐ _____
- ☐ _____
- ☐ _____
- ☐ _____
- ☐ _____
- ☐ _____

Self-Care
- ☐ _____
- ☐ _____
- ☐ _____
- ☐ _____
- ☐ _____
- ☐ _____

Health & wellbeing

Hours of sleep
Sleep tracker: ○ ○ ○ ○ ○ ○ ○ ○ ○ ○
                      1 2 3 4 5 6 7 8 9 10

Exercise
Time: _____

Activity: _____

Today's Water intake
🥛🥛🥛🥛🥛🥛🥛🥛

Shade in

MEALS

B ....
L ....
D ....

MY ACHIEVEMENTS TODAY

☾ EVENING REFLECTIONS

RATE MY DAY:

Daily Wellness Journal

Date: ___/___/20___   Sun Mon Tue Wed Thu Fri Sat

GRATEFUL for: _____

Today I CHOOSE TO FEEL

Today's GOOD HABITS

Things I do well
- ☐ _____
- ☐ _____
- ☐ _____
- ☐ _____
- ☐ _____
- ☐ _____

Self-Care
- ☐ _____
- ☐ _____
- ☐ _____
- ☐ _____
- ☐ _____
- ☐ _____

Health & wellbeing

Hours of sleep
Sleep tracker: ○ ○ ○ ○ ○ ○ ○ ○ ○ ○
1 2 3 4 5 6 7 8 9 10

Exercise
Time: _____

Activity: _____

Today's Water intake
🥛 🥛 🥛 🥛 🥛 🥛 🥛 🥛
Shade in

MEALS
B ···
L ···
D ···

MY ACHIEVEMENTS TODAY

EVENING REFLECTIONS

RATE MY DAY:

Thank you for your purchase

Check out the other range of journals available

Don't forget to leave a review. Thank you :)

INSPIRATIONAL JOURNALS

Designed with you in mind

Copyright 2019 – P.J. Clarke
All rights reserved. No part of this book may be reproduced or transmitted in any form or by any means, including but not limited to information and retrieval systems, electronic, mechanical, photocopy, recording, etc. without written permission from the copyright holder.